UNPLUG

BREATHE

CREATE

A MONTH OF GRANTING
YOURSELF PERMISSION
TO BE CREATIVE
THROUGH MEDITATION

Unplug Breathe Create: A Month of Granting Yourself Permission to be Creative Through Meditation is a work of my own creation.

The information in this book was correct at the time of publication, and the Author does not assume any liability for loss or damage caused by errors or omissions, again, this is my perspective, opinion, and experience, so it has been written as such.

Copyright © 2023 by megs thompson

ISBN - 978-1-961185-08-1

Cover, Book Design, and Layout by megs thompson, megswrites llc
www.megswrites.com

www.inomniaparatuspublishing.com

"SOMETIMES TO BE CREATIVE YOU HAVE TO GIVE YOURSELF PERMISSION TO NOT BE OUTSTANDING."

—JAMES K.A. SMITH

This journal is part of the
UNPLUG BREATHE CREATE
series & designed to be used
alongside a bespoke guided
meditation.

Download this month's meditation
using the QR code below:

HOW TO BEST USE THIS JOURNAL & MEDITATION

UNPLUG

The first step to reconnecting with ourselves as creative beings is to unplug & disconnect even temporarily from the countless electronic tethers that keep us firmly held in the world of shoulds & must's.

BREATHE

Take a few deep breaths, paying close attention to the way oxygen moves through your mouth & nose, filling your lungs & reawakening the creative genius locked safely within you, exhaling any fears, hesitations, or doubts that may filter your magic.

CREATE

Release your desire to control, plan & perfect every step & movement you make. Embrace the often wild, messy & chaotic magic that comes with allowing your inner creative to explore & play. Prepare yourself to experience fulfillment & satisfaction in new & creative ways.

DAILY ROUTINE

While moving through your day, begin implementing the use of affirmations. Both habits & beliefs are formed & strengthened through consistent repetition & before you know it your thoughts will become truths.

Included below are powerful affirmations that when paired with your daily tasks & activities, will empower you through this month of finding & claiming your own creative space.

I recommend repeating one or more of these affirmations aloud anytime you find yourself in front of a mirror, washing your hands, or refilling your beverage of choice.

I HAVE THE PERMISSION & FREEDOM TO MAKE MY CREATIVITY A PRIORITY.

I AM A POWERFUL, NATURALLY CREATIVE BEING.

I TAKE MESSY & IMPERFECT ACTION WITH EXCITEMENT & PRIDE.

30-DAY ENERGY TRACKER

When you've completed your daily meditation, make note of a single word or phrase that best describes your energy level in that moment.

Day 1	Day 2	Day 3	Day 4	Day 5
Day 6	Day 7	Day 8	Day 9	Day 10
Day 11	Day 12	Day 13	Day 14	Day 15
Day 16	Day 17	Day 18	Day 19	Day 20
Day 21	Day 22	Day 23	Day 24	Day 25
Day 26	Day 27	Day 28	Day 29	Day 30

DAY 1

During the meditation you found yourself in a long hallway. Describe that here in as much detail as possible. What does it look like? How does it smell? Where is it located? What color is the curtain at the end of the hallway?

_____

_____

_____

_____

_____

_____

_____

_____

_____

_____

_____

_____

_____

_____

_____

_____

_____

_____

ON A SCALE OF 1-5 WHAT'S YOUR
CURRENT CREATIVITY LEVEL?

DAY 2

Reflecting on the meditation, what did you see affixed to the cork board at the end of your hallway? Are there different modalities of your creativity or primarily one form? Did you recognize any of the pieces as creations from you past?

_____

_____

_____

_____

_____

_____

_____

_____

_____

_____

_____

_____

_____

_____

_____

_____

_____

ON A SCALE OF 1-5 WHAT'S YOUR
CURRENT CREATIVITY LEVEL?

DAY 3

Now, let's focus on one of the creative pieces that filled the cork board within your mediation. Describe just one of those here, in as much detail as possible. Was this something you created in the past, present, or future? How did seeing this piece make you feel? Do you recall how you felt while creating it?

ON A SCALE OF 1-5 WHAT'S YOUR
CURRENT CREATIVITY LEVEL?

DAY 4

Let's focus on another of the creative pieces that filled the cork board within your mediation. Describe just one of those here, in as much detail as possible. Was this something you created in the past, present, or future? How did seeing this piece make you feel? Do you recall how you felt while creating it?

_____

_____

_____

_____

_____

_____

_____

_____

_____

_____

_____

_____

_____

_____

_____

_____

_____

ON A SCALE OF 1-5 WHAT'S YOUR
CURRENT CREATIVITY LEVEL?

DAY 5

Let's focus on another of the creative pieces that filled the cork board within your mediation. Describe just one of those here, in as much detail as possible. Was this something you created in the past, present, or future? How did seeing this piece make you feel? Do you recall how you felt while creating it?

_____

_____

_____

_____

_____

_____

_____

_____

_____

_____

_____

_____

_____

_____

_____

_____

ON A SCALE OF 1-5 WHAT'S YOUR
CURRENT CREATIVITY LEVEL?

DAY 6

Let's focus on another of the creative pieces that filled the cork board within your mediation. Describe just one of those here, in as much detail as possible. Was this something you created in the past, present, or future? How did seeing this piece make you feel? Do you recall how you felt while creating it?

ON A SCALE OF 1-5 WHAT'S YOUR
CURRENT CREATIVITY LEVEL?

DAY 7

Let's focus on one more of the creative pieces that filled the cork board within your mediation. Describe just one of those here, in as much detail as possible. Was this something you created in the past, present, or future? How did seeing this piece make you feel? Do you recall how you felt while creating it?

ON A SCALE OF 1-5 WHAT'S YOUR
CURRENT CREATIVITY LEVEL?

DAY 8

Spend a few moments reflecting on when in your life you feel the most creative? Is this within your personal or professional life? How often are you able to enjoy this time?

_____

_____

_____

_____

_____

_____

_____

_____

_____

_____

_____

_____

_____

_____

_____

ON A SCALE OF 1-5 WHAT'S YOUR
CURRENT CREATIVITY LEVEL?

DAY 9

When was the last time you felt creative? Where were you? What were you doing? Who were you with? How can you bring more of this into your daily life?

DAY 10

Spend a few moments thinking about the past week. What experiences, obligations or tasks did you prioritize over exploring your own creativity? Could these tasks have been completed at another time? Are you able to set a date for yourself, even if for only 30 minutes, a few times a week, to pursue your creative outlets?

_____

_____

_____

_____

_____

_____

_____

_____

_____

_____

_____

_____

_____

ON A SCALE OF 1-5 WHAT'S YOUR
CURRENT CREATIVITY LEVEL?

DAY 11

How did you most enjoy expressing yourself creatively as a child? Is that something you might still enjoy today?

_____
_____
_____
_____
_____
_____
_____
_____
_____
_____
_____
_____
_____
_____
_____
_____
_____
_____
_____
_____

ON A SCALE OF 1-5 WHAT'S YOUR
CURRENT CREATIVITY LEVEL?

DAY 12

Close your eyes. Take 3 deep breaths & ask yourself, how do I want to explore my creativity today? What answer do you receive? How comfortable are you with trusting your intuition to guide your creativity?

ON A SCALE OF 1-5 WHAT'S YOUR
CURRENT CREATIVITY LEVEL?

DAY 13

What is one task that you complete every day. This may be something mundane, administrative & without much sparkle. How can you approach this task from a more creative standpoint?

_____

_____

_____

_____

_____

_____

_____

_____

_____

_____

_____

_____

_____

_____

_____

_____

ON A SCALE OF 1-5 WHAT'S YOUR
CURRENT CREATIVITY LEVEL?

DAY 14

How often do you allow yourself to embrace your own creativity? What's holding you back from prioritizing this time? As with any habit or skill, consistent repetition strengthens & solidifies your confidence as a creative being. Are you able to set aside 10, 20, or even 30 minutes each day to explore your creativity?

_____
....
_____
....
_____
....
_____
....
_____
....
_____
....
_____
....
_____
....
_____

ON A SCALE OF 1-5 WHAT'S YOUR
CURRENT CREATIVITY LEVEL?

DAY 15

What lights you up? What topics or areas in life are you most passionate about? How do you currently use your creativity in these areas? How might you be able to better tap into your creativity?

_____
_____
_____
_____
_____
_____
_____
_____
_____
_____
_____
_____
_____
_____
_____
_____
_____
_____
_____

ON A SCALE OF 1-5 WHAT'S YOUR
CURRENT CREATIVITY LEVEL?

DAY 16

Failure is a part of life, it's also part of the creative process. When did you last fail during a creative project? Focus on the fact that while the outcome may have fallen short of your intention, it was temporary & there is no reason to not try again.

_____

_____

_____

_____

_____

_____

_____

_____

_____

_____

_____

_____

_____

_____

_____

ON A SCALE OF 1-5 WHAT'S YOUR
CURRENT CREATIVITY LEVEL?

DAY 17

Where do you feel the most resistance when it comes to embracing your own creativity? Are these feelings based in past experiences or assumptions?

_____

_____

_____

_____

_____

_____

_____

_____

_____

_____

_____

_____

_____

_____

_____

_____

ON A SCALE OF 1-5 WHAT'S YOUR
CURRENT CREATIVITY LEVEL?

DAY 18

As children, we're naturally curious & willing to try new things, getting creative even when it may be uncomfortable. How can you grant yourself permission to embrace your childlike curiosity & creativity now?

_____

_____

....

....

....

_____

....

_____

_____

....

....

_____

_____

....

....

ON A SCALE OF 1-5 WHAT'S YOUR
CURRENT CREATIVITY LEVEL?

DAY 19

Spend a few moments journaling about creative projects, ventures & experiences that you'd like to explore. Make a plan for how you're going to pursue at least one of these creations within the next 30 days.

_____

_____

_____

_____

_____

_____

_____

_____

_____

_____

_____

_____

_____

_____

_____

_____

_____

_____

_____

ON A SCALE OF 1-5 WHAT'S YOUR CURRENT CREATIVITY LEVEL?

DAY 20

During the meditation you found yourself within a
safe, creative space. Somewhere you feel
comfortable, creative, empowered & safe. Describe
that space in as much detail as possible. Is there a
place within your life that resembles your creative
space? Is it somewhere you visit often? Grant
yourself permission to revisit this place physically,
to reconnect & prioritize your own creative genius.

ON A SCALE OF 1-5 WHAT'S YOUR
CURRENT CREATIVITY LEVEL?

DAY 21

What places, people, things, scents, tastes, or memories inspire your creativity? How can you connect with these influences more regularly?

ON A SCALE OF 1-5 WHAT'S YOUR
CURRENT CREATIVITY LEVEL?

DAY 23

What are your favorite forms of creative expression?
This may be words, music, paint, food, dance, clay,
wood, steel, yarn, etc. When was the last time you
took an afternoon to enjoy this creative outlet?

ON A SCALE OF 1-5 WHAT'S YOUR
CURRENT CREATIVITY LEVEL?

DAY 24

If you were to write yourself a permission slip,
granting you the time & space to explore your natural
creativity, what would it say? Spend a few moments
journaling below. Now, using your favorite medium
(pens, paint, crayons, fabric, rocks, string, words, etc),
create a permission slip of your own & be sure to
position it somewhere you'll be able to see it
throughout the day as a reminder.

_____

_____

_____

_____

_____

_____

_____

_____

_____

_____

_____

_____

_____

_____

ON A SCALE OF 1-5 WHAT'S YOUR
CURRENT CREATIVITY LEVEL?

DAY 25

What do you consider to be your unique creative
strengths? How would you describe these strengths
to others? Are these skills you were taught by
someone else or through self-discovery?

_____

_____

_____

_____

_____

_____

_____

_____

_____

_____

_____

_____

_____

_____

_____

_____

ON A SCALE OF 1-5 WHAT'S YOUR
CURRENT CREATIVITY LEVEL?

DAY 26

What creative projects or ideas have you wanted to
pursue, but decided against? What reasons have kept
you from exploring these projects further? Are they
related to cost, experience level, fear, etc?

....

....

....

_____

_____

....

....

....

_____

_____

....

....

....

_____

_____

....

....

ON A SCALE OF 1-5 WHAT'S YOUR
CURRENT CREATIVITY LEVEL?

DAY 27

When was the last time you felt stuck or stifled in regard to your creative expression? What was stopping you? Was it an outside force, perceived judgement from others, or your own limiting beliefs?

ON A SCALE OF 1-5 WHAT'S YOUR
CURRENT CREATIVITY LEVEL?

DAY 28

Do you have a space in your home where you feel most creative? A space where you're able to unplug, breathe & create freely? This may be a spare room, a closet with a desk, or a corner near a window. How often do you utilize this space?

....

....

....

_____

_____

....

....

....

_____

_____

....

....

....

_____

_____

....

....

ON A SCALE OF 1-5 WHAT'S YOUR
CURRENT CREATIVITY LEVEL?

DAY 29

Have you ever created a vision or mood board? How about a creative inspiration board? What images, colors, patterns, words, feelings, etc would you include on your board? Why? What is it about these items that inspires you creatively?

ON A SCALE OF 1-5 WHAT'S YOUR
CURRENT CREATIVITY LEVEL?

DAY 30

How might you introduce yourself to a new acquaintance in a more creative way? Perhaps through a short story, a poem, a picture, a graphic, a song, or something else?

_____

_____

_____

_____

_____

_____

_____

_____

_____

_____

_____

_____

_____

_____

_____

ON A SCALE OF 1-5 WHAT'S YOUR CURRENT CREATIVITY LEVEL?

If you already have an
UNPLUG BREATHE CREATE
subscription, keep an eye on your
mailbox for your next delivery.

If you aren't yet a member but
would like to be, or are
interested in gifting a
membership to someone else,
scan the QR code below.

www.ingramcontent.com/pod-product-compliance
Lightning Source LLC
Chambersburg PA
CBHW071217120626
46546CB00006B/2612